The Knee Book

The Knee Book

Everything You Need to Know About Knee Disorders, Treatment Options, and Maintenance Programs

Howard Kiernan, M.D.

Director of Orthopedic Clinics, Chief of the Knee Clinic, Columbia Presbyterian Medical Center; Assistant Professor of Orthopedic Surgery, Columbia University College of Physicians and Surgeons

Illustrations by Michael Trossman

Crown Publishers, Inc.
New York

Published by Crown Publishers, Inc.,
201 East 50th Street, New York, New York 10022.
Member of the Crown Publishing Group.

Random House, Inc. New York, Toronto, London, Sydney, Auckland

CROWN is a trademark of Crown Publishers, Inc.

Manufactured in the United States of America

Design by Studio 131

Library of Congress Cataloging-in-Publication Data

Kiernan, Howard
The knee book: everything you need to know about knee disorders,
treatment options, and maintenance programs/ by Howard Kiernan;
illustrations by Michael Trossman.
p.   cm.
1. Knee—Care and hygiene.   2. Knee-Wounds and injuries.
3. Knee—Diseases.   I. Title.

RD561.K495   1995

616.5'82—dc20   94-44846

ISBN 0-517-59889-2

10   9   8   7   6   5   4   3   2   1

First Edition

CONTENTS

Preface   7

1 Our Most Commonly Injured Joint   10

2 How the Knee Joint Works   14

3 Conditioning Exercises   28

4 Acute Injuries   40

5 Braces, Balms, and Whirlpools   53

6 Chronic Arthritis   65

7 Reconstructive Surgery   76

8 Prevention and Maintenance   88

Index   95

PREFACE

In the movie *Claire's Knee*, a bearded diplomat in his late thirties, about to settle down and get married, becomes obsessed with an eighteen-year-old girl—or, rather, with the eighteen-year-old girl's knee. "In every woman there is a vulnerable point," he says. "For some, it is the nape of the neck, the waist, the hand. For Claire in that position, in that light, it was the knee. It was the magnet of my desire. The precise point where, if I could follow this desire, I would put my hand." The diplomat is French and, as we all know, the French can be relied on for refined and exotic tastes when it comes to the ways of love. But even for a Frenchman the knee is a perverse choice. And of course therein lies the joke.

Bony and knobby and unprepossessing, the knee is a part of the body that most of us tend to view with reservations, if not outright distaste. In a recent article in *Vogue,* the supermodel Christy Turlington confided to an interviewer, "I don't like my knees very much. Not that they're bad necessarily, but Linda has very nice knees." At the same time, Linda Evangelista, a fellow supermodel and the possessor of those "nice knees," was ready to do away with them entirely. "I have the most hideous knees," she said with the assurance of someone who knows her own mind.

When it comes to the knee, handsome actors fare no better than beautiful models. Wearing striped pants and a cutaway, Hugh Grant cuts a dashing figure in *Four Weddings and a Funeral.* Wearing Bermuda shorts, he is just another goofy, loosely thrown together, perenially late bachelor.

But homely as the knee may be, and much as we may like to disparage and make fun of it, we cannot do without it. We rely on it with every step we take.

This is a short book intended for readers who have knee joint injuries and for those who wish to avoid them. It will explain how the knee functions and explore the causes of knee joint pain and knee joint instability. It will then show what can be done to treat these problems and how to prevent them.

I first became interested in orthopedics in high school, when I fractured a bone in my knee playing football. Over the next few years I broke two more bones—an ankle and an elbow—and grew to have more than a passing acquaintance with our friendly neighborhood orthopedist. But I really fell in love with orthopedics and trauma surgery in medical school. As a resident at Columbia Presbyterian Medical Center in New York City I worked with Dr. Frank Stinchfield, a world-famous hip surgeon. After spending an extra year training with him on hips, I was invited by

Dr. Stinchfield to join the staff. But not as a hip surgeon. "We already have one of them," he said, smiling. "You're going to do *knees*."

So, with Dr. Stinchfield's backing I was sent around the country to see how knee surgery was done at other medical centers. This was in the old days when most orthopedists did just about everything and almost no one concentrated on a single joint. Today most orthopedists spend their entire careers concentrating on just one area, whether it is joint replacement, sports medicine, or hand surgery. Gone are those days when an orthopedist would deal with virtually any injury or disease affecting the musculoskeletal system.

Since July 1974 I have been practicing orthopedic surgery at Columbia Presbyterian Medical Center. There we have a large orthopedic clinic, where one day a week I run a clinic for the treatment of injuries and disorders of the lower extremities—not just knees but hips, feet, and ankles. My private practice now consists almost exclusively of injuries and disorders of the knee.

1

OUR MOST COMMONLY
INJURED JOINT

To everything there is a season, according to Ecclesiastes. But statistics show that no matter what the season we can always find ways to do serious injury to our knees.

Each fall New Yorkers succumb to marathon fever. Every morning in my office I see at least one patient who has been running two to three miles a day for his health, three times a week. Now he has caught the fever. He is running two to three miles every day and five to ten miles on the weekend. And he can barely walk. I say "he" because in my experience women are too smart to do something like that. Running rarely causes serious injury. More runners die because they get hit by a car than because they suffered a heart attack. Most running injuries are so-called overuse injuries. My patient is used to low mileage at a slow but steady pace. Suddenly he has increased his mileage threefold and has upped his pace. He has added a few hills and some uneven ground to his route and he has hit the perfect formula for a sore knee. He comes to see me because he has pain just under the kneecap and he can't sit behind the wheel of his car comfortably. Going down stairs is painful. And just a few weeks ago, he thought he was in great shape. He was.

Winter is ski season. Never been on skis before? Then head for the nearest slope, rent ski equipment, and hit the lift with some friends who really know how to ski. In my office I actually see more women than men who are injured this way. The patient's ski tip has caught the snow. The bindings don't release. She twists her knee, hears a "pop," and falls down. When she tries to get up, her knee buckles and she falls down again. She has to be taken off the slope by the ski patrol. Four hours later, her knee is the size of a watermelon. This is a serious injury.

Come spring I see an injury that has nothing to do with sports. It is time for my patient to bring his daughter's stuff home from her college dorm. Her room is three flights up. College campuses are built for kids, not adults. Two hours, ten trips, and at least a ton of stuff later, and his knees are killing him.

Summer affords everyone plenty of opportunity for injury, from basketball to ultimate Frisbee to volleyball to a bracing day in the surf. Last summer, I treated a patient who was swimming in heavy waves. When he made it past the big breakers, he figured he was home safe. He was standing in a foot and a half of water, with his foot buried in the sand, when he was hit from behind by a huge wave. There are a couple of tons of water in a good-size wave. He was knocked flat and in the bargain sustained a torn meniscus (what in lay terms is called torn cartilage).

The knee is the most commonly injured joint in the body, and at least half of the population between twenty-five and seventy-five has at one point been disabled by knee pain (only neck and back pain are more common). When all the disorders of the knee are considered, it is evident that more surgery is performed on the knee than on any other part of the body, including the back. Arthroscopy of the knee is the third most commonly performed operation in the United States; knee replacement is the fifth; menisectomy the seventh; and ligament repairs the fourteenth. Seventy-seven percent of all confirmed ligament injuries involve the cruciate ligaments.

With the tremendous increase in interest in physical fitness and sports, knee injuries have become a major health concern. Whether their cause is traumatic, inflammatory, or degenerative, knee disorders affect men and women of all age groups.

We will begin with a look at how the knee is constructed. In treating—or avoiding—knee pain and instability, it is crucial to know how the joint works under normal conditions and how it fails to work after an acute injury or with chronic disease. In the chapters that follow, we will examine how the joint fails to work when there is chronic disease or after an acute injury. Most knee problems can be overcome with simple exercises and with braces. Since the majority of knee problems are mechanical in origin, medicines are rarely needed. But when medicines are needed, it is terribly important to use the right one. I will discuss the types of drugs used to treat knee problems and when they are indicated. Next, I will describe in detail the two major operations that are done for knee disorders: arthroscopy and joint replacement. The last chapter of the book is devoted to a maintenance program for the knee. If all goes well, the surgical procedures described will never have to be implemented.

2

HOW THE KNEE JOINT WORKS

Think of the last time you missed the final step on a dark stairwell. That sudden jarring you experienced is an exaggeration of what happens every time your foot hits the floor. Our bodies have been cleverly constructed to absorb such impact loads with a minimum of damage to our frame. The musculoskeletal system enables us to run, walk, jump, carry, and throw with a minimum of effort through a system of levers.

These levers are the bones connected at the joints and moved by the muscles. The knee is a perfect example of such a lever system. The thighbone, or femur, is joined to the tibia, or shinbone, at the knee. The knee is a lever with the fulcrum at one end, the effort-arm close to the fulcrum, and the resistance way out at the other end. This is a third-class lever system. (Other examples of third-class levers at work are a hammer driving a nail and fly-fishing.) Such a lever system is ideal for running and kicking because it maximizes the effect of the powerful quadriceps muscle in moving the foot very rapidly; however, it is a disadvantage in stair climbing and squatting because your body weight is at the wrong end.

Rather, what happens in these types of activities is very much like lifting a brick with a tennis racket. For this type of activity the lever system is all wrong, which is why many people experience pain going up and down stairs. Curiously enough, it takes more work to go down stairs than up because the muscles must not only lift your body weight down the height of the step but must also break the momentum of your body weight falling down the step.

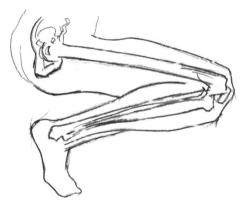

Anatomical knee joint in a deep squat.

This lever system can work to your disadvantage as well. I have treated a man in his late sixties who was playing softball in the rain with much younger members of his large office staff. He was caught in a rundown and slipped in the muddy base path, completely rupturing not one but both of his thigh muscles. Bummer!

The powerful thigh muscles move the tibia and the femur. Our word "muscle" actually comes from the Latin word for little mouse because of the appearance of most muscles—muscles have a body, a snout by which they attach to one bone, and then a long tendon or tail by which they attach to another bone. The pairs of muscles acting across any joint are evenly balanced and are referred to as the agonist and the antagonist. The muscle that shortens to straighten a joint is the agonist and the muscle that simultaneously lengthens to allow the joint to move is the antagonist. If we didn't have this system of evenly balanced agonist and antagonist muscles, we would move with a jerky mechanical motion like a puppet. A muscle's ability to move a joint comes from both its size and from the distance of its attachment to the joint. The larger the muscle, the more force it can generate. If the muscle is attached at a distance from the joint, it has more leverage and can generate more force (much like the way a child can balance an adult's weight if the adult sits close to the fulcrum of a seesaw and the child sits out at the end).

A tall priest was walking down a grassy slope on the grounds of his retreat house one night. Although he had done this a thousand times before, the grass was wet and he had forgotten about the six-inch curb that marked the border between the grass and the driveway. He missed the curb and his foot slipped on the wet grass. His heel caught on the curb and down he went so that he wound up sitting on his heel and fracturing his kneecap. The enormous leverage afforded by the length of his thigh and shin literally pulled the kneecap apart like a soda cracker.

Hamstring muscles are much smaller than quadriceps

in cross-sectional area, but they are inserted farther down on the tibia and therefore have a greater mechanical advantage than the quadriceps. As a result these two muscle groups are evenly matched. This is a very important protection mechanism for the joint. It ensures that the force around and across the joint will be in balance and not excessive.

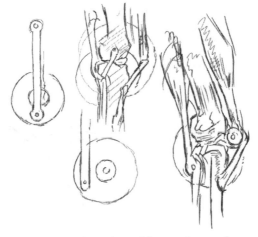

Mechanical analog of hamstring and quadriceps muscle action.

Hamstring muscle pulls are fairly common in sports. Keith Hernandez, the great Mets first baseman, was sidelined for weeks with a hamstring pull, which he got stretching to catch a ball. Eventually that injury ended his career. Hurdlers usually get hamstring pulls when they think they have cleared the bar with their heel and at the last minute they try to kick over the bar, only to strain the hamstring and sometimes even pull it off its attachment to the pelvis. Pete Sampras tore his hamstring tendons in a Davis Cup singles match and didn't even realize it until the next day. He won the match, but had to withdraw from the final.

The muscles are the principal shock-absorbing mechanism of the body. They absorb about 60 percent of the energy of impact. When you jump off a low wall, you assume the "jump position" with your hips and knees flexed to receive the impact of the fall. I had a patient who was changing an overhead lightbulb in his kitchen late one night, missed the last rung of his stepladder, and landed with enough force to fracture his heel. The surprise of missing the step caught him off guard, not giving him enough time to flex his knees as he should have. Our body depends on muscles to do most of the impact absorption. Your muscles do exactly the same thing in a much less dramatic way whenever your heel hits the ground during normal walking. Restoring muscle strength after an injury or strengthening normal muscles after a long period of inactivity is essential. For example, before going skiing in the winter, you should spend at least eight weeks getting your legs in shape if you want to protect yourself from injury.

The nervous system also has an elaborate system of position sensors, called proprioceptors, that tell it exactly where your arms and legs are in space at any time. It takes six years for this proprioceptive sense to develop fully, which is why toddlers take so long to learn to walk. Because of proprioception, we can walk and run without looking at our feet. Just as a cat will land on its feet if dropped upside down, so will we right ourselves if we trip or step on uneven ground. Inside the joints, these sensors protect the joint from undue stress and strain. (This is why you cry "uncle!" when your arm is twisted—the perception that your shoulder is about to go out of place forces you to give in.) It is this elaborate interplay between the muscles and the joint position sensors that enables us to run, jump, and fall without injury.

There are three bones in the knee joint: the femur, the tibia, and the kneecap, or patella. The patella is actually part of the quadriceps muscle, embedded in the tendon or tail of the muscle. The patella protects the front of the knee. It also improves the mechanical efficiency of the quadriceps muscle, because the mechanical advantage of a muscle is directly related to the distance of its line of action from the axis of the joint. The patella almost doubles the distance of the quadriceps from the center of the knee joint.

The importance of the patella has been underscored by the practice of "kneecapping" by political and underworld activists (terrorists and gangsters). A broken kneecap is not fatal but the recovery period is long enough for the victim to think long and hard about why these people were so upset with him. It can take a person a year or more to recover from a broken patella. The assault on the skater Nancy Kerrigan, which was an attempt to fracture her kneecap, introduced Mafia tactics to the squeaky clean

Olympics. We (doctors and laymen alike) always think first of the bone when someone "breaks a leg." But a fracture is a soft tissue injury in which a bone has been broken. The kneecap will heal in six weeks, but the entire leg—muscle, ligaments, cartilage, and skin—will take twelve months or more to mend. Kerrigan recovered so quickly not only because she was in such superb physical shape but because it was a bungled assault. A real pro could have finished her career.

In-line skating can have the same effect. Wearing these new skates with in-line wheels, you can get going at about thirty miles per hour. Most people are used to skates with four wheels, which are much more stable and not as fast. The best way to protect yourself from injury is to wear lots of body armor and learn how to skate. The body armor consists of protection for the elbows, wrists, and kneecaps. Unfortunately, pedestrians don't wear body armor. It can be horrifying to be on a city sidewalk on a weekend and have to dodge people on in-line skates careening down the sidewalk totally out of control. Actually, almost as many people are injured by 150-pound in-line skaters gone amok as are injured on skates.

The other two bones of the knee provide the structural framework for the weight-bearing function of the lower limb. The femur has rounded ends to allow it to roll over the surface of the tibia, which is slightly dished to conform to the end of the femur. In fact, the conformity is not that close. The fit is more like a cup in a saucer, which—for anyone who has ever carried a cup in a saucer knows—is a very unstable arrangement. This is the reason that the knee is so frequently injured. It is an intrinsically unstable joint, and any movement that involves twisting may disrupt it. Unfortunately, most of the activities of living involve some sort of pivoting off the leg and foot. Even something as trivial as crushing a cigarette butt with your heel acts against the basic motion of the joint.

I have taken care of a young father who was playing with his infant son on the ground. He was slightly off balance when he picked the boy up from a crouching position. He heard a pop, felt a sharp, stabbing pain, and could not straighten his knee. This seemingly trivial injury had crushed the cartilage in his knee. A similar thing happened to a tall, long-legged friend of mine who was getting out of his low-slung sports car in a crowded parking lot. In pivoting out of the front seat, he managed to crush his meniscus.

I am not suggesting that you don't play on the floor with babies or ride in sports cars, but these two incidents give you an idea of the magnitude of the forces involved.

Skiing is the major cause of knee ligament injuries in the United States. Most skiing injuries involve twisting when the bindings don't release. This is like crushing a butt with a crowbar on your foot at 30 mph! No wonder the ligaments give way.

The femur, the strongest bone in the body, is the major weight-bearing bone in the leg. It is shaped like a double-ended champagne flute, with a narrow center and two flares at the ends. The narrow pipelike center bears the weight of the leg. The flared ends are constructed so that they attenuate the shock of impact loading, much like the champagne flute's capacity to keep the champagne from sloshing out of the glass.

The knee is a hinge joint, which allows simple bending because of the rounded shape of the femur (the "cup," in my earlier analogy) and dished shape of the tibia (the "saucer"). The shape of the opposing surfaces of the bones in a joint determine the amount of flexion. The femur is more curved than the tibia and this mismatch is compensated for by the meniscus. The meniscus is commonly referred to as the cartilage (when an athlete injures the meniscus, the press reports it as a cartilage injury). This confusion goes back to the days when microscopes were not refined enough to distinguish between the meniscus and true cartilage, also called hyaline cartilage ("hyaline" means glassy or transparent).

The shape of the bones has more to do with the function of the knee than determining the amount of movement of the joint. The rounded, or convex, mate in a joint is stiffer than the dished, or concave, side. This makes for more even distribution of the stresses. Furthermore, the ends of the bone are covered with true cartilage, which is a very complex shock absorber. In contrast to the meniscus, which is a woven fibrous disc like a doormat, true cartilage is a fine mesh of protein strands like the framework of a sponge. These protein strands are called collagen. Within this framework are large molecules called proteoglycans. When you step on cartilage, the proteoglycans are squeezed out of the mesh, absorbing considerable energy, much the way water drains out of a wet sponge when it is pressed. Unlike a sponge, where the water is lost, the proteoglycans are electrically attracted to the collagen mesh, so when your weight is lifted from the cartilage, the proteoglycans are drawn back into the mesh and are ready to function again.

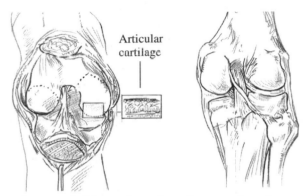

Articular cartilage

Shock absorbing action of cartilage and meniscus.

The meniscus is made entirely of collagen strands in a basket-weave pattern. This arrangement enables the meniscus to absorb loads in all directions. The most common load on the human knee is compression, which happens when the femur is forced against the tibia (for example, each time you step on a stair). The most damaging loads are shearing forces that result when you pivot or twist off your leg. I have treated a patient who kicked what looked like an empty paper bag on the sidewalk outside his office. It turned out to have a brick inside of it, so he tore his meniscus in the process. The meniscus acts as a spacer between the tibia and the femur because, as I have mentioned, the ends of those bones are not a perfect match. The meniscus also allows for the efficient circulation of the joint fluid, or lubricating fluid, between the bones. This creates a well-lubricated low-friction bearing in the joint. Joint fluid is made by the lining (or synovial) cells, to nourish and lubricate the cartilage.

Tensile or distracting forces are resisted by the ligaments and tendons. This happens when you get your foot stuck in deep mud or caught in something like a ski binding. The ligaments and tendons keep the knee from coming apart as you pull your foot out of the mud or ski binding. Sometimes, however, the force is so great that the ligaments and tendons are overwhelmed. That is when the ski patrol must be called upon to come and get you.

A well-known actor saw me after he hurt his leg falling off a motorcycle. Actually he was sitting on the bike in his driveway when it began to topple; in his effort to extricate his leg, he pulled his hamstring tendons. If you contract your muscles in an explosive way like that, you generate a force of almost 90 percent of the muscle's capacity, which is quite close to the tensile strength of the ligaments and can pull them apart.

Ligaments are different from tendons in that ligaments connect two bones together and tendons connect muscles to bones. There are four ligaments in the knee. The two collateral ligaments are located on either side of the joint and control its simple hinge motion. The ligament on the inside of the knee is called the medial collateral and the one on the outside is called the lateral collateral ligament. These ligaments also prevent the bones in the knee from slipping from side to side. Because they resist this motion, they are the most commonly injured in sports where the knee is forced in a direction opposite to its plane of motion—clipping in football is a good example.

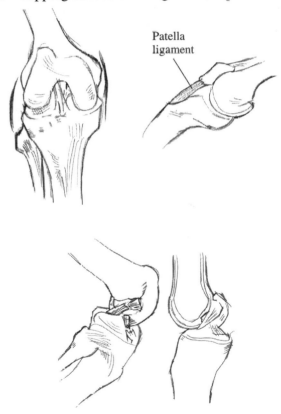

Patella ligament

The ligament system of the knee.

The other two ligaments in the knee are the cruciate ligaments. Located inside the joint, they prevent the tibia from sliding in front of or behind the femur. The anterior cruciate attaches to the front of the tibia, while the posterior cruciate ligament attaches behind it. Of the two, the anterior cruciate ligament is the one most commonly injured in skiing. In my office we often see "big bump, hard landing" injuries. The "big bump, hard landing" occurs when your skis hit an obstruction on the slope and you go flying up in the air and land sitting on your heels. Here the protective contraction of the powerful quadriceps muscle pulls the anterior cruciate ligament. Volleyball players are particularly susceptible to this kind of injury. Coming down from an explosive jump to spike a ball, if they are accidentally bumped by a teammate, they can pull the cruciate ligament apart. They hear a pop. The tibia

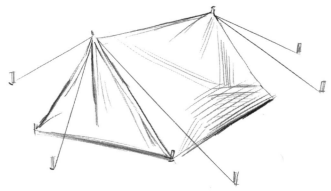

The tent analogy.

feels as if it has separated from the femur. The knee swells suddenly and they can't finish the game.

The interplay of the muscles, ligaments, cartilage, and bone in the knee has been compared to a well-pitched tent. Like the tent poles, the bones resist compression and the muscles and ligaments resist tension; all work in concert to keep the canvas of the tent up, even in a pretty stiff breeze.

The knee, then, functions to provide the body with purposeful motion through the interplay of the bones, cartilage, ligaments, and muscles. It is a well-lubricated bearing designed to minimize stress and strain on the body as a whole.

3

CONDITIONING EXERCISES

Malcolm Forbes's grandson once caught him doing leg lifts in his study. He thought, What is this old man trying to do? Impress people with his muscles? When he asked Forbes, "What are you doing that for?" Forbes replied, "When I stop my motorcycle at a light, I'm not so sure anymore that I can put my leg out and hold it up."

Did you ever wonder how athletes like Joe Namath or Dick Butkus could play grinding professional football on knees with no ligaments and no cartilage left? The answer is that they had enormously powerful leg muscles. In fact the number of injuries in sports such as football has been dramatically reduced by the introduction of better equipment and the emphasis on preseason conditioning. The same conditioning techniques can be applied in preparation for recreational sports, especially with seasonal sports such as skiing. Going out on the slopes with deconditioned muscles after a long period of inactivity is inviting injury. The same is true with soccer, rugby, and lacrosse. The majority of injuries suffered in recreational activities such as basketball and the racket games are muscle strains and tears, and not the more serious ligament and cartilage injuries. Nonetheless, these injuries can result in a significant loss of time and may result in poor performance following return to that sport.

A good conditioning program should include stretching and strengthening exercises. However, the best preparation for any sport is practicing the actual activity itself. Pitching baseballs is a far better practice for a baseball pitcher than lifting barbells.

The value of stretching is largely a matter of opinion, with no conclusive proof one way or the other. On a theoretical basis, stretching should make a difference. Stretching increases the range of motion of the joints, and the warm-up period increases muscle temperature. The collagen framework in our muscles is like taffy. It becomes more elastic with an increase in temperature. Also like taffy, it will stretch more with a slow sustained pull than with a hard jerk. This property is called viscoelasticity.

Stretching sets the muscle-tendon units at the optimum length and thereby increases the efficiency of the muscle contractions. Although this should exert a protective effect, studies have not shown a reduced incidence of injury or postexercise muscle soreness. However, the warm-up and stretching protocols in the various studies were all different. It is my belief that stretching—if properly done—does have a protective effect. The principal difference between the studies that showed a beneficial effect from stretching and those that did not was the duration of each individual stretch and the total length of time that the muscles are stretched. In the studies that advocate stretching, the subjects held each stretch for one minute and stretched for no more than five minutes. The muscles being stretched are held in tension bordering on slight discomfort. The muscles stretched for the legs—the hip flexors, quadriceps, hamstrings, gastrocnemius, and soleus—are depicted in the following diagrams.

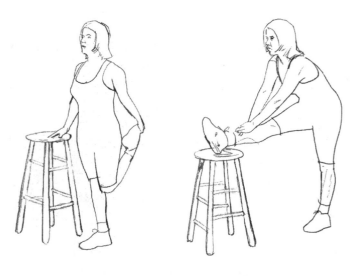

Hip flexor and quadriceps stretch.　　　　**Hamstring stretch.**

These stretching exercises are for general conditioning and are good for anyone. Ballistic stretching exercises like jumping jacks have no value. They simply activate the stretch receptors in the muscles, cause them to *contract*—

Gastroc stretch.

the opposite effect of that intended, which is to *stretch* the muscles and tendons. Also, ballistic exercises apply short, sharp loads to the muscles and tendons, both of which stretch better if slow, sustained loads are applied.

Resistive strengthening exercises are described as isometric, isotonic, variable resistance, and isokinetic. The purpose of these exercises is to increase muscle strength, power, and endurance. Each of these programs has advantages and disadvantages.

In an isometric exercise, your muscles develop tension without moving, such as when you push as hard as you can against a wall. This type of exercise can be done at several different angles in the range of motion of the joint being exercised, such as with your knee straight and with it bent at a right angle. Strength is the measure of the muscle's ability to develop tension. Maximum strength gains can be made by tightening the muscle about 90 percent as hard as you can, holding that for about six seconds and repeating that three to five times. The exercise is even more effective if you repeat it at several different points in the arc of motion of the joint. The obvious advantage is that you can do these exercises anywhere and they require no special equipment.

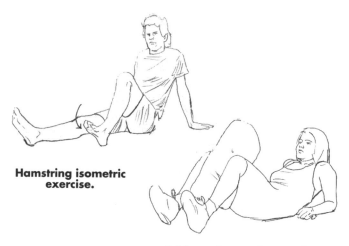

Hamstring isometric exercise.

Adductor isometric exercise.

The disadvantage is that you are doing no work because the muscle is not moving, and therefore you will not develop any endurance. Endurance is the measure of the muscle's ability to do work or move a weight through

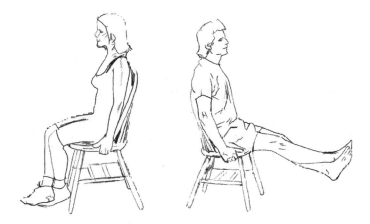

Quadriceps isometric exercise.

Hip flexor isometric exercise.

a distance, like working out with a barbell. Some effective isometric exercises for the knee are illustrated in the diagrams on pages 32–33.

Weight lifting, the kind of exercise most people think of when you mention exercise, is an isotonic exercise. Your muscles are doing work both raising and lowering a barbell. When your muscles lift the weight, they shorten; this is called a concentric contraction. When you lower the weight, your muscles lengthen but are also developing tension called an eccentric contraction.

Thomas DeLorme popularized these exercises at the end of World War II as a method of rehabilitation for injured soldiers. He was one of the first physicians to do this. DeLorme was not only an orthopedic surgeon but also an Olympic weight lifter. His progressive resistance program was based on the 10 resistance maximum (RM), the maximum amount of weight that a person could lift ten times. His recommendation was to start with one half of the maximum weight, progress to three quarters of the maximum, and then lift the maximum weight in three successive sets of ten repetitions. You then try to increase your maximum weight. The more weight you lift, the greater the strength you gain. The more repetitions you do, the more you accomplish and the more endurance you develop. The advantage of this type of program is that it requires little equipment and will develop both strength and endurance. The disadvantage is that you can only work at slow speeds and therefore can't gain much power. (In this context, power is the amount of work done in a certain time or the rate at which the work is done.)

Another disadvantage of weight lifting concerns load and resistance. Although the most effective strenthening programs load the muscles moving the joints through the full range of motion available to those joints, with barbells the resistance is provided at the start or at the end of the motion—not at both ends. In addition, the resistance offered by the barbells varies through the arc of motion because of the leverage provided by the joint. This causes sticking points, where the resistance is too heavy at some points in the arc and therefore too light at others. As a result, only a small portion of the muscle is worked heavily, with the rest of the muscle being exercised lightly or not at all.

Despite these limitations, progressive resistance exercises have been used successfully for fifty years. Muscle

Squat exercise for thighs.

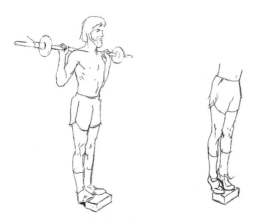

Heel raises for gastroc.

Knee extensions for quadriceps.

Knee curls for hamstrings.

strength and power are gained through heavy resistance and few repetitions. Endurance is developed through low resistance and many repetitions. Illustrated on page 35 and on the top of the opposite page are examples of isotonic exercises for the knee using free weights. For safety reasons, you should start with 70 percent of the maximum resistance.

The rest interval between sets should be 60 to 70 seconds. The exercises with your feet on the ground are called closed kinetic chain exercises and are more effective because they more closely simulate the normal interplay of the agonist and antagonist muscles. Exercises with the foot off the ground are called open kinetic chain exercises and mostly load the agonist muscles. With open chain exercises, you have to perform the motion in a smooth manner so as not to jam the joint at the end of the arc of motion. You can begin to add weight when the repetitions become easy. Increasing the weight is the heart of a progressive resistance program.

Variable resistance programs are designed to overcome the theoretical shortcomings of the isometric exercises. The most well known is the Nautilus system, which uses specially designed machines that vary the resistance through the arc of motion as the leverage of the muscles moving the joint changes. This allows you to exercise through the full range of motion of the joint and to work the muscles concentrically and eccentrically. The disadvantage is that you have to have access to these expensive machines. The Nautilus machine can be used for leg extension, leg curls, hip abduction, hip adduction, and calf raises. When starting out, use a light weight so that you can do the exercise in a proper manner. You should do the repetitions through a full range of motion, raising on a 1-2 count and lowering on a 1-2-3-4 count. Do the repetitions in a smooth and controlled manner without jerking. Pause briefly at the fully contracted and starting position to maximize the muscle contraction at the extremes of motion. You should be able to do at least eight good repetitions. If you can't, the weight is too heavy. If you can do twelve or more, then the weight is too light and you should add another plate of five or ten pounds.

Unlike the progressive resistance and variable resistance exercise programs, in which the resistance is applied with weights, isokinetic training applies loads to the muscles by controlling the velocity of the lever arm at which you exercise. The lever moves at a fixed rate. You push and pull against the lever and can exercise both the agonist and antagonist muscles. However, all the contractions are concentric. You can exercise the muscles through the full range of motion. An additional advantage is that you can exercise at both slow and fast speeds. The most well known of these machines is the Cybex. These machines can be used for leg extension, leg flexion, leg press, and squat. For an eight-week program, you can set the leg extension and leg flexion machines at 120 deg./sec., leg press at 120 deg./sec., and the squat machine at 60 deg./sec. You can then decrease the velocity every two weeks to increase the force you have to exert to complete the repetition. Usually two sets of each exercise for a total of twenty-five minutes three times a week is sufficient for most purposes.

If all you want is strength gains, isometrics are fine; however, if you want to build endurance, you should do resistance exercises. In the end, it doesn't make any difference whether you work out at home with free weights, go to the gym to use the Nautilus equipment, or go to a therapist and work on a Cybex—at the end of eight weeks the results will be the same. So you pay your money and take your choice!

Jogging, treadmill running, cross-country ski machines, exercise bicycles, and walking are intended to increase cardiovascular endurance. Since the muscles are moved against little resistance, the strength gains are small but the aim is to develop greater endurance. In order to get the desired effect, at least twenty to thirty minutes of continuous activity is necessary. The intensity of the workout should raise your heart rate to 70 to 85 percent of your maximum heart rate (your maximum heart rate is 220 minus your age). You should do these exercises every other day for at least 20 minutes.

A combination of stretching, strengthening, and endurance exercises should reduce the chances of your being injured in recreational sports.

4

ACUTE INJURIES

A celebrated poet who is an avid tennis player started to play volleyball. Tennis requires short stops and starts and lateral running movements, while volleyball is mostly jumping. The first time he played, his knees were sore the next day, but in forty-eight hours he was all better. The next time, his knees were sore for two days and it was a whole week before he was back to normal. The following time he played, he was lame for a week and it was several weeks before he was back playing tennis, *not* volleyball. If you intend to play a new sport with the same enthusiasm you play your favorite sport, you have to do some cross training. Or just not try so hard.

Fortunately, most of the knee injuries we suffer are muscle strains and minor ligament injuries. The most important feature of more serious trauma is swelling of the joint within the first four hours of the incident. The blood contains a protein called fibrinogen, which causes it to clot. The synovial lining of the joint prevents fibrinogen from getting inside of the knee. If any serious injury has occurred, there is immediate bleeding and subsequent swelling. A swollen knee within the first four hours usually means that you have torn the meniscus or a cruciate ligament, or fractured one of the bones in the joint. This is *not* something to treat at home—you should see a doctor.

The majority of knee complaints resolve themselves in a month to six weeks and can be managed with a little common sense. You can usually figure out what caused the problem and how to avoid it in the future.

Half the patients I see in our knee clinic have some complaint of pain around the kneecap or in the front of their knee. This was usually caused by such activities as walking up or down stairs carrying a heavy object, kneeling in the garden or on a hard floor, and running, especially down hills. There was no specific injury and none of the sudden pain or swelling that characterizes a serious injury. Now the pain is made worse by stair climbing, walking down an incline, or sitting still for any period of time—for instance, in a theater or in a car. True swelling and locking are not present, but the patient has the sense that his knee might give way, especially when going down a step. This complex symptom has been called chondromalacia for want of a better name. Chondromalacia refers to a softening of the cartilage layer behind the kneecap. Actually, this is only one of many reasons that people have anterior knee pain.

Recently, I saw a woman in the office who had been working in her garden planting tulips. She told me she planted the tulips while kneeling on the ground and that the bulbs were in a sack behind her. To get a bulb she would pivot around on her knees and then pivot back to plant them. The first day she worked for a total of four hours in the garden and had no trouble, but the next day going up and down the subway stairs was impossible. In this patient's case, kneeling and sitting on her heels put great pressure on the back of the kneecap, and then the pivoting back and forth created a shearing force that injured the cartilage and caused chondromalacia.

Oddly enough, the conditions that cause pain in the front of the knee are age related. Youngsters at the time of the growth spurt attending puberty can have pain at the insertion of the patella tendon on the tibia. This is called Osgood-Schlatter disease. Not really a disease at all, this condition results from the way the muscles and tendons keep up with the rapidly growing child's skeleton. The muscles insert by way of the tendons into bones at specialized locations called apophyses. The apophyses are made of bone with a soft cartilage cap to allow for expansion during growth. If the skeleton has a sudden growth spurt the muscles and tendons may lag behind and begin to pull the soft cartilage cap off the apophysis.

The cartilage cap rarely gets pulled off completely, so aside from the temporary pain and disability, Osgood-Schlatter does not lead to any long-term problems. However, it is a nuisance for the active teenager who wants to play soccer or basketball, or engage in any running or jumping sport that puts tension on the patella tendon. We used to treat this condition with immobilization in a stovepipe cast for six weeks. This didn't help much because the skeleton continues to grow in girls until they are about fifteen and in boys until they are about nineteen. All the immobilization did was to cause muscle weakness, so this type of treatment has been abandoned.

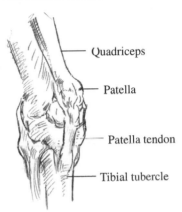

Quadriceps

Patella

Patella tendon

Tibial tubercle

The extensor mechanism.

Osgood-Schlatter disease, jumper's knee, and quadriceps tears are all disorders of the quadriceps muscle. The quadriceps muscle is the large muscle running from the hip to the tibia that straightens the knee joint. The largest muscle in the body, it acts like a pulley in that it runs in a groove in the femur much like the rope runs through the pulley of a block and tackle. Injuries such as these are age related. Teenagers get Osgood-Schlatter disease, young adults get jumper's knee, middle-aged adults are more likely to get early arthritis of the patella, and older adults get partial tears of the quadriceps tendon.

Not too long ago, when I still qualified as a middle-aged adult, I was carrying a carton of medical journals out to the car to be bound. My wife can't stand the sight of these cluttering up the house, so at the end of each year, off they go to the bookbinder. I was crossing the street carrying a big carton and noticed a half second too late that someone had not cleaned up after his dog. In a desperate effort not to step in the mess, I overstepped the curb and down I went, straining my quadriceps muscle in the process.

The best treatment for Osgood-Schlatter is to rest the knee when it is really painful and to apply ice to the tibial tubercle. A simple neoprene knee sleeve, which can be purchased in any sporting goods store, will relieve the pressure on the patella tendon. In addition, patella straps, called Levine or Chopat straps, accomplish the same purpose. Osgood-Schlatter disease is a self-limited condition that disappears at the completion of skeletal growth, and there is no reason to restrict the activities of teenagers because of it.

Young adults also get a chronic patella tendonitis called jumper's knee. High-impact aerobic exercises, running, and jumping sports such as basketball are the usual culprits. This can prove to be more of a problem than Osgood-Schlatter because it is not self-limited and is not part of the normal growing process of the skeleton. Jumper's knee is actually a partial tear of the patella tendon caused by repetitive strain. Tendons will heal on their own if allowed to rest, but it is very hard to rest the patella tendon: every step you take puts considerable strain on it. Just walking at a slow speed, the load on your patella tendon is one third of your body weight (for instance, if you weigh 150 pounds, that is a 50-pound load). Going down stairs, the load is 3.5 times your body weight. And squatting is 7.5 times your body weight. So you can see that the normal activities we take for granted put large loads on our knees. With jumper's knee you have to put the knee to rest until the tenderness is gone. This does not mean immobilization but simply avoiding for the moment those activities that precipitated the tendonitis. Ice and compression with an Ace bandage or knee sleeve will help relieve the pain, and isometric exercises with the knee in extension will prevent muscle atrophy until the tendonitis resolves.

Patients I see in the clinic for pain behind the kneecap fall into two groups. The larger consists of teenagers and young adults who have anterior knee pain, or chondromalacia, which comes from the soft tissue in front of the joint. This is not arthritis and does not lead to arthritis. The second group consists of middle-aged and older patients who do have arthritis. (I will discuss the treatment of chronic arthritis in chapter 6.) The symptom that brings both groups to the doctor is the same—pain in front of the knee—but there are important differences. The younger patients have pain after strenuous activity that includes running and jumping. They may hear a peculiar grating sound behind the kneecap as they go up and down stairs and feel as if the knee may give out on them. However, they don't have any true locking or giving way. They don't have any symptoms that indicate arthritis, such as swelling, night pain, and weather ache. The knee joint is a "soft tissue" joint despite the fact that there are three bones in it. Most of the energy of impact is absorbed by the muscles and tendons. And this energy is considerable. For instance, if a 150-pound man walks a mile, he takes 2110 steps and his knees sustain a load of 63.5 tons. If he runs a mile he takes only 1175 steps but his knees absorb a load of 110 tons. And the muscles and tendons absorb the lion's share of the work. Minor stretching and tearing of the soft tissues is the cause of the pain in chondromalacia.

Seventy percent or more of chondromalacia patients get better by strengthening the muscles about the knee to improve the energy-absorbing capacity of the soft tissues. If you watch someone running from behind, you can see a shock wave move up the leg each time the heel hits the ground. This is the effect of the leg muscles absorbing the shock of impact.

Neoprene knee sleeves help as well. Your muscles are 70 percent water and the sleeve is a semirigid container encompassing the semifluid contents of the muscles. The sleeve acts like a hydraulic shock absorber, much like an air bag in a car. This is why many professional tennis players now wear bicycle shorts, which function exactly the same way.

The sudden violent contracture of a muscle such as the powerful quadriceps muscle can actually pull muscles and bones apart. If you deliberately contract a muscle, you can generate about 50 percent of the force the muscle is capable of producing. If you catch your heel on the edge of a step and reflexively contract your muscles in an effort to keep from falling down the stairs, you will generate about 90 percent of the force of the muscle—this is enough to pull the muscle or attached bone apart. People in their forties or fifties are likely to fracture the patella in this way. I saw an older lawyer who commuted to work by subway. On a particularly snowy day, she was on the D train, standing in a puddle of melted snow. The train lurched forward and, in an effort to keep her balance on the slippery, moving floor, she contracted her muscles and popped her patella in half. People in their sixties or seventies are more likely to rupture the quadriceps tendon. Unfortunately, all of these injuries require surgical repair.

More serious knee injuries are characterized by traumatic incident, followed immediately by pain and within four hours by swelling. Eighty-five percent of the time the injury is a torn ligament, a torn meniscus, or a broken bone inside the knee. The other 15 percent of the time you are lucky and have only torn the lining of the knee; this will heal in a short time. In the more serious injuries, you usually hear a snap or pop and are then unable to stand on the leg. Within four hours the knee is quite swollen and painful. Icing the knee helps. Taking aspirin or any of the other nonsteroidal pain medications only increases the bleeding, so in this situation don't take them. Tylenol is probably the best for the pain and then it is time to rush to the orthopedist.

The meniscus has layers to it and can split horizontally along the layers like a piece of plywood when the glue dries and the wood buckles. Or the meniscus can tear at right angles as if you were cutting plywood with a band saw. These tears are called parrot beak or bucket-handle tears. The laminar or horizontal tears cause symptoms because the meniscus is supposed to absorb shock and the delaminated meniscus is no longer an effective shock absorber. Although the meniscus will never heal, the lost shock-absorbing function can be compensated for by strengthening the muscles about the knee.

Powerful muscle forces in contracting quadriceps.

Once you have a vertical or right-angle tear in the meniscus, the torn piece behaves like a hangnail and gets caught between the tibia and the femur and causes true

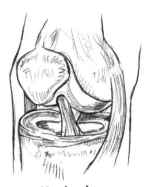

Meniscal tear.

locking. Again this tear will never heal. The reason a torn meniscus and torn cruciate ligaments never heal is that the linings of joints exclude the protein called fibrinogen from entering the joint. Fibrinogen is the Krazy Glue of the body and is necessary for wound healing. But you wouldn't put Krazy Glue in a joint because it would never move again, and so nature doesn't either. The best treatment for parrot beak or bucket-handle meniscal tears is dependent upon the size of the tear. If they are small, the preferred procedure is to snip them off like a hangnail. If they are large and still attached to the blood supply, it is best to sew them back. Both of these operations can be done arthroscopically as an outpatient procedure. The recovery time is about six weeks.

Ligament injuries are a little more complicated. Of the four ligaments in the knee, the two that are most commonly torn are the medial ligament and the anterior cruciate ligament. Remember, it is the cruciate ligament that is torn 77 percent of the time. Ligaments are torn in some sort of twisting motion, such as when a ski binding does not release.

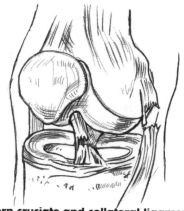

Torn cruciate and collateral ligament.

I treated a patient who had been waterskiing in the Hudson River. A lot of flotsam winds up in that river, including creosote-soaked telephone poles and railroad ties. These things float about six inches under the water, so they are hard to see. He hit one of these poles at 35 mph—and wrecked his knee, tearing all his ligaments, needless to say. The medial collateral ligament is outside of the knee joint. When it is torn, fibrinogen is deposited at the injury site. The ligament will heal if protected for six weeks. The cruciate ligaments are inside the joint. Fibrinogen is excluded from the injury site and the tear will never heal regardless of how long it is protected.

This does not mean that all torn cruciate ligaments

have to be repaired surgically. The function of the cruciate ligaments is to hold the tibia in contact with the femur. A person with a torn cruciate ligament has a "trick knee" that can give out without warning. This is usually caused by pivoting off the affected leg. However, only about one third of patients with a torn cruciate ligament really have such an unpredictable knee that they require surgery. The majority of people with a torn cruciate can compensate for normal activities with muscle-strengthening exercises and by wearing a brace for sports. People who are engaged in sports that require jumping or pushing off—like volley-ball, basketball, or skiing—will still have trouble. If you have an old cruciate ligament injury, you know how your knee will behave when you are participating in these sports. Therefore, in such a case, the decision to have surgery or to work on exercises and wear a brace is pretty clear-cut.

The real problem is what to do with an acute injury. How do you know whether the knee will be stable enough in the future to do pretty much what you want or whether you should have the ligament reconstructed? This is a tough decision for everyone to make, including the so-called experts. If your favorite recreational activities or your occupation doesn't necessitate much jumping and pivoting, then you can probably get by with the brace and exercises. However, if you have to rely on a stable knee, then it is best to bite the bullet and have the ligament reconstructed. Even if you decide not to have the surgery right then, the results are the same if the reconstruction is done later, provided that you don't incur a second injury in the meantime. (This is where knee injuries get their deservedly bad reputation, by the way. If your knee has been weakened by one injury, you are more likely to be injured a second time in a more trivial incident.)

The situation with fractures about the knee is more straightforward. I was treating a motorcycle cop some years ago who had stopped a woman on the New York State Thruway for speeding. He parked his motorcycle behind her car, wrote the ticket, and then returned to his motorcycle. She threw her car into reverse and pinned him to his cycle, breaking the end of his femur in the process. To restore the anatomy of his knee we had to use screws and a plate. Anyone who has ever been stopped by a motorcycle cop and entertained this particular revenge fantasy would do best not to give into it.

If one or more of the bones of the knee joint is fractured, the bone fragments may be separated. If the fragments are not displaced, all you have to do is immobilize the knee until the fracture heals. This usually takes six weeks. If the fragments are separated, then they have to be reassembled and held together with screws and wires. Of course, don't try this at home!

5

BRACES, BALMS, AND WHIRLPOOLS

Once you have injured your knee, you are dealing with muscles and ligaments that are stretched and torn. If the injury is serious, there may also be torn cartilage and broken bones. All of this damage results in bleeding, swelling, muscle spasm, and pain. As soon as possible, you want to begin therapeutic exercises to regain use of your knee. The goal of any therapeutic exercise program is to prevent muscle atrophy and to restore muscle strength, muscle endurance, and joint motion.

The injured tissues must be protected and held in place so that they can heal. The amount of immobilization required depends on the amount of damage suffered. For a simple contusion, an Ace bandage for a day or two will suffice. For a broken kneecap, a plaster cast for six weeks may be necessary. Unfortunately, prolonged immobilization can cause atrophy, or wasting, of the muscles and bone. It can also cause loss of normal elasticity in the ligaments and tendons. Ideally, immobilization should permit early restoration of joint motion and normal function of muscles and ligaments. With a variety of splints and braces, we are able to provide something called protective mobilization.

When I was in the service, I was a navy doctor assigned to the marines. One of the rifle companies had an orange tom for a mascot and the cat would sleep in the barracks with the men. One night, a marine accidentally stepped on the sleeping cat with his heavy combat boot, breaking the cat's hind leg. They brought the injured cat to my sick bay. Of course, I didn't have a clue as to what to do, so I called the division vet. "You don't have to do a thing," he said. "Cats are much smarter than people. Just put him in a small room with his food and litter box and he will limp around on three legs until the fracture has healed enough for him to walk on all four." This is protective mobilization.

RICE is the acronym commonly used for rest, ice, compression, and elevation—the four things you should do for a sprain or contusion to relieve pain and muscle spasm and to limit bleeding and swelling. The simplest immobilizer is an Ace compression bandage, familiar to anyone who has ever sprained an ankle. This elastic compression bandage is adequate for a simple sprain in which only a few muscle or tendon fibers have been torn and the knee is still stable. Once the bleeding has stopped, after about forty-eight hours, the compression bandage can be discarded.

As I said earlier, neoprene knee sleeves, like those worn by basketball players, are very effective hydraulic shock absorbers. Your muscles are 70 percent water. By acting as a semirigid container for the fluid contents of your muscles, the knee sleeve absorbs much of the energy of impact when your heel hits the ground in running and walking. For the sleeve to be effective, the fit must be snug. Immediately after an injury, a sleeve may be too snug to wear without pain. Here the Ace compression bandage has an advantage.

Nonetheless, because Ace bandages tend to unravel, once the acute pain has gone, most people find the knee sleeve more effective. Some sleeves have a hole in the center and some don't. With most designs it doesn't make any difference. The hole is there to help you center the sleeve on the knee. If you have a dislocated kneecap, there are sleeves on the market that incorporate a horseshoe-shaped pad to encircle the kneecap and keep it from dislocating. Some sleeves have metal side bars with hinges; they are there to keep the shape of the sleeve, just like the tabs in a shirt collar. These bars on a sleeve don't provide much stability, and if your knee is unstable, you need a more substantial brace.

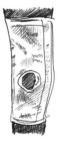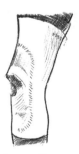

Neoprene knee sleeve with patella restraint.

Once a sufficient number of muscle or tendon fibers have been torn, the joint becomes unstable, and a more substantial splint is needed. The canvas knee immobilizer with Velcro straps is well known to anyone who has been skiing—by the end of the afternoon, you can see plenty of them in the parking lot outside the first-aid station. Knee immobilizers have metal stays in the canvas and will stabilize the most serious of ligament injuries and even some fractures. They don't allow any knee movement, and this loss of motion causes the surrounding muscles to atrophy very quickly. Most of the atrophy occurs within the first two weeks, but it takes months to reverse. The immobilizer can be used as a resting splint, which you can remove very easily to do exercises to regain knee motion and to prevent muscle atrophy.

These simple splints are useful if the knee injury doesn't require more than two weeks of immobilization. If more protection is necessary, off-the-shelf hinged rehabilitative splints allow the knee to move while protecting the healing muscles and tendons. The knee ordinarily moves in an eccentric arc, more like a cam than a wheel. The hinge on these braces mimics the knee joint's camlike arc of motion, which allows the injured joint to function normally. You can't walk or run in these braces because they are held together by Velcro fasteners. Velcro makes it easy to get the braces on and off for exercise, but it doesn't provide enough stability for functional activities.

Functional braces are designed to stabilize an injured knee during activities like walking and running and prevent further injury. The functional brace was made famous when Joe Namath won the Super Bowl in the Lenox Hill Derotation Brace. There are many functional braces—both off-the-shelf and custom models—on the market today. Functional braces come in two basic designs, both of which rely on a post-and-hinge system. One has a thigh and calf shell and the other has thigh and calf straps to suspend the brace on the leg. In most studies, the post-and-hinge/shell design performs better.

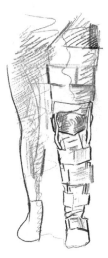

Knee immobilizer.

Nevertheless, the tibia doesn't have to move very much on the femur to make the knee buckle—half an inch is enough. Any functional brace would have to be bolted to your leg to prevent that. None of these braces can eliminate the shifting of the tibia on the femur that occurs in sports. Only muscle rehabilitation in concert with bracing will work. This is what Namath did. Most patients feel a subjective improvement when wearing the brace. And athletes who haven't completely rehabilitated their muscles do better in the brace. But complete muscle rehabilitation is still the key to stability.

Unloading brace for bowleg.

If you have a bowleg or knock-knees, there are braces designed to straighten the knee and unload the painful side. Again, muscle rehabilitation is the key to alleviating pain and improving function.

In the first few days following injury, pain, swelling, and muscle spasm prevent motion of the injured knee. If the injury is not too severe, these symptoms quickly subside and full motion is restored. It must be noted that until such motion has returned, any muscle-strengthening program may not be effective. Restoring motion is the first order of business. With the more severe injuries, a physical therapist can make an enormous difference in shortening disability time. Therapists frequently employ heat, cold, massage, and hydrotherapy to facilitate the healing process.

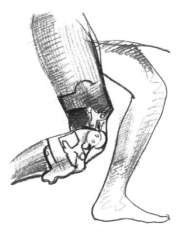

Functional brace.

Cryotherapy, or the application of cold following an injury, reduces swelling by causing contraction of the blood vessels. By slowing down the metabolism of the cooled tissues, this prevents pain and muscle spasm. Nerves are particularly sensitive to cold. By slowing the metabolism of the pain fibers, cold applications are a very effective analgesic. That is why trainers apply ice to a batter hit by a pitch. The motor nerves to the spastic muscles are also partially paralyzed, reducing the spasm. Cold penetrates deeper than heat and its effects last longer. Ice, frozen gels, and immersing the leg in cold water are the most common ways to apply cold. If you are doing this at home, be sure to wrap the ice or gel in a towel and apply it for no longer than ten to fifteen minutes. There are two reasons for this. First, cold can injure tissues. Second, after fifteen minutes your blood vessels dilate to prevent frostbite and the extremity begins to warm up—the opposite of what you wanted! Cryotherapy is good for acute injuries because it reduces pain and swelling, but it makes proteins such as collagen stiffer. So it is no good for chronic injuries where joint contractures have formed. It can also be dangerous for people who have vascular disease, diabetes, or loss of normal skin sensation.

Heat causes increased blood flow to the injured area. The increased blood flow brings in the white blood cells and other scavengers to get rid of the damaged tissue and blood clots. Since it also causes more swelling, heat is not helpful in the first forty-eight hours, when active bleeding is taking place. It is much more useful in the later phases of healing. Heat also increases the elasticity of proteins in the tendons and ligaments and helps restore motion. Heat can be applied directly (with a heating pad) or by convection (with a heat lamp) or with diathermy. Diathermy produces heat deep in the tissues by converting energy in one of three ways. Short-wave diathermy converts the energy of high-frequency current; microwave diathermy uses electromagnetic radiation; and ultrasound diathermy converts high-frequency acoustic vibrations.

Hot applications are most effective at 40 to 45°C (104 to 113°F) for twenty to thirty minutes. Thermal damage to the proteins begins to occur at 46°C (155°F). Most patients find moist heat to be more relaxing than dry heat. Lower, longer-lasting applications are most effective, so hot packs are better than hot towels and hot water bottles, which lose their heat rapidly. A hot pack contains a silicone gel that is heated in a hydrocolator. They should always be placed on top of the part treated, not under it, to prevent burns.

Directly applied heat penetrates only about 1 cm (less than ½ inch). Diathermy penetrates more deeply. Tissues with higher water content, such as muscle, are more affected by diathermy than fat or skin. Ultrasound penetrates fat better than short waves or microwaves, so it is used more often in the leg. Short-wave or microwave diathermy is usually applied for ten to twenty minutes. Like short-wave and microwave diathermy, ultrasound is applied through a coupling medium such as mineral oil for three to five minutes. Ultrasound is absorbed by the proteins of muscle and bone and is able to increase the permeability of cell membranes. Therefore, it can be used to transport substances such as cortisone to these tissues. This process, which is called phonophoresis, is an effective way to reduce inflammation.

In applying heat, people who have peripheral vascular disease or loss of skin sensation must be careful. Heat can also cause dehydration. Short waves and microwaves can cause hot spots around metal plates and other implants in the leg, so care must be used. This is less likely to happen with ultrasound.

Massage can decrease swelling and mobilize contracted tissue. Analgesic balms and liniments are actually skin irritants that increase blood flow to the injured area, causing a feeling of warmth. Thus, the analgesic effect is really produced by counterirritation. Whirlpools are the most commonly used form of hydrotherapy for the leg. In addition to heating the leg, they make it possible for active exercise to be done at the same time. Repeated immersions in hot water followed by cold water are helpful in reducing edema—this is called a contrast bath.

Electrical stimulation is helpful in retraining atrophied muscles. High-voltage short-duration direct current is applied to the muscle. The electrical stimulation of the muscle helps the rehabilitiation because patients get a feeling for what they are supposed to be doing as they exercise. Direct current is also capable of transporting chemical substances like steroids deep into the tissues. This is called iontophoresis. In fact, it is preferable to administer steroids by phonophoresis or iontophoresis because you don't get the side effects, such as weight gain or tendon rupture, that are associated with taking them orally or by injection. Another application of electrotherapy is the TENS units used to control acute and chronic pain. These are small, battery-powered transcutaneous electrical nerve stimulators that apply high-frequency short-duration pulses, so that the pain fibers are preferentially stimulated over the motor fibers. This has the effect of jamming the pain control center in the brain.

All of these methods can be used to help regain motion in a knee following injury or in a knee that is stiff and painful because of a chronic condition. Once motion is restored, muscle strength can be restored by using the exercises described in chapter 3. However, be extremely careful not to place too much stress across an injured joint.

The most commonly used program for strengthening employs free weights with isotonic concentric contractions lifting the weights against gravity, and eccentric contractions returning the weights to the starting position. When exercising a muscle, you must push the muscle to the point of fatigue if you expect to gain strength. Fatigue pain occurs during and just after the exercise period. Delayed pain occurs twenty-four to forty-eight hours after the exercise period and is the result of microscopic tears in the muscle. This may be prevented by postexercise stretching. If pain arises from the injured joint *during* the exercise, you have to cut back on the program. Joint pain forces the brain to inhibit the muscles acting over the joint and has a negative effect. If the muscles are too weak to exercise with weights, a modified program can be started with heavy rubber tubing, similar to Bunsen burner tubing. Then you can progress to free weights.

If you have access to a pool, water-based exercise is another way to start strengthening a painful knee. Water is an ideal medium for exercise. The body is buoyed up by the water, resulting in less stress and pressure on the bones, ligaments, tendons, and joint. You can do the same resistive exercises in waist-deep water using the resistance created by the viscosity and drag of the water, which is proportional to the effort exerted. This has been called "aquacise." Aqua running or deep-water running is simulated running in the deep end of the pool as you wear a life vest. No contact is made with the bottom of the pool, but you run just as you would on land. This removes any impact loading but provides a specific method for maintaining cardiovascular fitness while recovering. This type of exercise may well be available at your local Y.

In isokinetic training, the muscle contracts at a constant speed and develops maximal tension at all knee joint angles. This type of training is excellent for strength gains but may put too great a stress on the injured joint in the early stages of healing. This type of training has to be done on machines that maintain a constant rate of change of the knee joint angle either by hydraulic resistance (like the Orthotron) or electrical resistance (like the Cybex).

Endurance is gained through the use of friction machines such as stationary exercise bicycles and cross-country ski machines. The greatest gains in endurance are made with high repetition and low loads. This program has to be adapted to each situation but, in general, pain and fatigue should be the guide for progress through successive stages. By following this program you should be able to head off the chronic condition I will discuss in the next chapter.

6

CHRONIC ARTHRITIS

When we refer to arthritis as chronic, we are speaking of pain, swelling, or stiffness in a joint for more than six months. Half a year is enough time for any acute injury to heal. Up to this point we have been discussing mechanical injuries. Mechanical injuries are best treated first with rest, ice, an Ace bandage, and elevation and then with exercises to regain strength and motion. Rarely are anti-inflammatory drugs needed. Simple pain relievers help you to do the exercises to get the motion back.

In chronic conditions, you are dealing with either the accumulated damage of repeated injury or inflammatory arthritis. The two large classes of arthritis are degenerative arthritis and inflammatory arthritis. The former is also called osteoarthritis.

Degenerative arthritis is "wear and tear" arthritis, involving damage to a joint that occurs over time and with use. This is also called traumatic arthritis. If you drive over a nail on the highway, you wind up with a flat tire. If you continue to ride the rim, you wind up with a bent wheel and finally a broken axle. So too with injuries to the knee. If you tear a ligament, the knee becomes unstable. This can be corrected with exercises and bracing. The second time you injure the same knee, the meniscus is often damaged as well. Now the knee is even more susceptible. The next injury leads to a chip in the cartilage covering the end of the femur, and this is the beginning of degenerative arthritis. The harder the knee has been used, the more likely it is to be damaged. Chronological age hasn't that much to do with it. In addition to repeated injury to the knee, the second major cause of degenerative arthritis is malalignment of the knee. Most people are born with straight legs and their weight is carried equally on both sides of the knee.

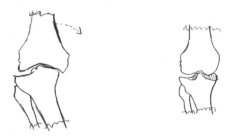

Mechanical effect of bowleg.

Mechanical effect of knock-knees.

However, if you have bowlegs or knock-knees, the weight is loaded too much on one side of the knee.

This is like riding on a tire that is out of alignment. The tread on one side will wear down and the tire will have a much shorter life span than the manufacturer has advertised. Most people who have their knees replaced are not ex–football players but people who were born with bowlegs or knock-knees. Just because you were born with legs that are not straight does not mean that you will develop degenerative arthritis. In fact, many athletic men and young boys have bowlegs because their muscular coordination developed early and they started standing and walking before the bones were strong enough to support their weight. When a well-coordinated man walks or runs, he can keep his center of gravity over the center of his supporting leg and thus the weight is evenly distributed. Many women have a slightly knock-kneed alignment because the female pelvis is wider than the male's to allow for birth. Again a well-coordinated woman can center her weight over her supporting leg. As we all get older, however, our muscular coordination and balance begin to fail and then one side or the other of the knee begins to bear a disproportionate share of the load. Therefore, we associate degenerative arthritis or osteoarthritis with old age, but actually it is the result of load bearing, not age.

The other major form of arthritis is inflammatory arthritis, a condition caused by factors inside the body. For some unknown reason the body turns against itself and begins to manufacture self-destructive antibodies. The most well-known example of an inflammatory arthritis is rheumatoid arthritis. Here the body's immune system creates antibodies that attack the cartilage in the joints. The joints with the most cartilage, like the hip and knee, are particularly susceptible. Rheumatoid arthritis also attacks the joints in the hand and wrist. Although these don't seem to be very large joints, the amount of cartilage they contain is large for their size. In fact the hallmark of this disease is the deformity of the hands.

Destruction of joint in inflammatory arthritis.

Oddly enough, rheumatoid arthritis is a modern disease. Sir Alfred Garrod was the first doctor to identify this disease as a new entity in the early nineteenth century. Since the disease affects the hands so characteristically, you would expect to see evidence of it in paintings before Garrod's description. But there is none. Although, for instance, evidence of tuberculosis was found in Egyptian mummies, no evidence of rheumatoid disease exists prior to the nineteenth century. Something happened at that time to trigger the human immune system. Some industrial pollutant, since it coincided with the onset of the Industrial Revolution? A virus? A bacteria? No one knows for sure and modern science has yet to identify the exact cause.

There is a family predisposition to the disease as well. Relatives of someone with rheumatoid arthritis are four times as likely to have the disease as anyone else. The treatment of inflammatory arthritis is mainly with medicines to relieve symptoms and to prevent joint destruction and deformity. This is why the market is flooded with so many anti-inflammatory medicines.

Immune reactions in rheumatoid arthritis.

The immune system of all patients with rheumatoid arthritis eventually produces an antibody called rheumatoid factor. This is actually an auto-antibody, because it reacts with the patient's own gamma globulin. This is how the factor is identified in the laboratory. Gamma globulin is a protein produced by the immune system to defend the body against invading bacteria and it will stick to such foreign objects. Because it will also adhere to latex particles, it is used in latex fixation, a common blood test to identify those with rheumatoid arthritis. Latex particles are coated with human gamma globulin and then mixed with the patient's serum. If rheumatoid factor is present, the latex particles will agglutinate, or stick together. This is a positive test and such patients are referred to as seropositive.

The disease is more severe in the presence of high levels of rheumatoid factor. The rheumatoid factor/gamma globulin complex then initiates the inflammatory response in the joint by damaging the patient's own white blood cells and precipitating the release of the other mediators of inflammation, such as the prostaglandins. This is where aspirin and other nonsteroid anti-inflammatory drugs help. They block the production and release of prostaglandins.

The patient's own lymphocytes also participate in the attack on the joint. The lymphocytes are white cells. We have two kinds of lymphocytes: T cells and B cells. The T cells are lymphocytes that are capable of recognizing foreign antigens. When a T cell recognizes a foreign antigen, it secretes chemical messengers called lymphokines, which then mobilize the B cell. The B cells are the lymphocytes that make the antibodies attack the foreign antigens. When T cells correctly identify foreign antigens, this process allows the body to fight back against an invader. However, when the T cells incorrectly tag a nonforeign cell as foreign, this same process triggers the autoimmune system.

Why do T cells turn against you? Infections frequently precipitate an autoimmune disease. Viruses and bacteria try to fool the immune system by making short chains of amino acids that look like they belong to the body (like faking the password in the army). In responding to the invader, the immune system can begin to attack itself by mistake. Researchers can cause a joint inflammation similar to rheumatoid arthritis in rats by immunizing them with tuberculosis bacteria, because of the similarity between the protein coat of the bacteria and the protein of the rat's cartilage.

Currently the anti-inflammatory drugs used to treat rheumatoid arthritis address the effect and not the cause and have their own side effects. In the future, the answer may be to create antibodies to block or remove the T cells involved, or to use irradiated T cells to vaccinate the patient to prevent the induction of the disease.

Autoimmune attack on articular cartilage.

These anti-inflammatory drugs that block prostaglandins are also effective in the treatment of gout. In gout, uric acid crystals cause the destruction of white cells and the release of prostaglandins, with similar effects on the joint. However, prostaglandins serve other, more positive functions in the body than fostering inflammation. They protect the stomach by reducing the amount of acid secretion and preventing acid reflux into the esophagus; they also control the blood flow in the kidney. Therefore, by blocking prostaglandin release, anti-inflammatory drugs have side effects—ulcers and kidney damage are possible, as are damage to the liver and interference with platelet function. Platelets are the little cell fragments that make the blood clot; by affecting platelet function, aspirin helps prevent heart attacks and strokes, but too much aspirin can cause bleeding.

When is a cortisone injection warranted? Cortisone got its bad reputation from its abuse in sports, especially football. The hero in Peter Gent's *North Dallas Forty* has his knee injected every day so he can play football. Of course, the injection takes the pain away temporarily so he can cause more damage to his knee (which is why doctors have abandoned this practice). However, cortisone has its place in an acute attack of rheumatoid arthritis and also in gout and pseudogout. If this is done no more than a few times a year, no harm will be done to the joint.

It usually takes a few days for the cortisone to take effect. When I was working with Dr. Frank Stinchfield, he would sometimes talk about his early adventures. At the end of World War II he was sent to Saudi Arabia to take care of King Ibn Saud's knee, toting enough equipment to perform surgery if necessary. But when his party arrived at the train station near the palace, the baggage was vandalized by some beggars. One kicked a hole in a crate of surgical equipment and was immediately arrested by the palace guards. The next day, when Stinchfield was presented to Ibn Saud, this beggar was dragged in and his foot was cut off right in front of everyone. "I knew right then and there that this guy meant business," said Stinchfield. "I'd have to be crazy to operate on him—if the surgery didn't work, he'd do the same to me." Cortisone had just come into use at the time, so Stinchfield told the king that he didn't need surgery. One shot ought to clear up his knee pain. But Ibn Saud was no fool. "How long will it take?" he asked. Stinchfield figured he'd say a couple of days to give himself enough time to clear out. The king said, "Fine— you will be my houseguest until my knee gets better." So Stinchfield spent the next few days driving around the countryside with Ibn Saud in his Rolls Royce. The king had a big sack of gold coins at his feet and he would drive from town to town tossing coins to the villagers who had come to greet him. Fortunately for Stinchfield, the cortisone worked like a charm. In a few days he was out of Saudi Arabia. But the problem with cortisone is that it always works for the first few days. It is only later that the pain returns.

With chronic arthritis the horse is out of the barn. Joint damage has already occurred. The aim now is to reduce symptoms and prevent further damage and deformity. In the acutely painful stages of both degenerative and inflammatory arthritis, rest is the most important step to reduce the pain and swelling. When the knee joint is swollen and painful, you feel most comfortable with the knee bent. But this will lead to a flexion contracture, which will prevent you from being able to fully straighten your knee. Splinting the knee in this stage helps a lot. Nobody likes the idea of using crutches, but at this point crutches may be necessary to take weight off the joint (a cane does not do the job here). Once the acute symptoms are under control, exercises to regain motion and muscle strength are started. Analgesics such as Tylenol or Darvon and modalities such as heat may be necessary to start the exercise program. Every effort should be made to prevent the formation of deformities. Once the deformities have become fixed, bracing is not effective.

Even though the knee joint has suffered damage, the situation is far from irreversible. With proper use of anti-inflammatory drugs and analgesics, exercises, and bracing, further damage can be prevented and function restored. Unfortunately, this can take several months and most people don't have much patience.

I was treating a woman in her mideighties for chronic arthritis of her knees. After a few weeks of exercise and analgesics, her knees were not much improved. She said to me, "When am I going to get better, Doctor?" I said that it would take several more weeks and she would just have to be patient and work on the exercises and thereby avoid surgery." "Patient," she said. "At this stage in my life, Doctor, I don't even buy green bananas!"

While we have not yet discovered the cause of chronic arthritis, there are encouraging signs in its treatment. Recently, researchers in Sweden have reported success using test-tube-grown cartilage cells to repair the knees of patients with degenerative arthritis. Healthy cartilage was taken from each subject, grown in tissue culture, and then reimplanted on the denuded part of the patient's arthritic knee. This study involved only a small number of patients and to date the follow-up period has not lasted long enough to tell if this method has any lasting merit, but this technique shows promise. It may be the answer for degenerative arthritis—not only in the knee but in any joint of the body.

7

RECONSTRUCTIVE SURGERY

Sometimes the best-laid plans come to naught or don't work out quite the way you expected. It could be that a course of exercises does not put a stop to acute knee pain and now your doctor tells you that you need surgery. Is it necessary? Will it hurt? How long will you be laid up? What can you expect? Will you be as good as new? Well, it depends on what is wrong. To go back to the flat tire analogy, if all you have done is run over a nail, a rubber plug will make your tire as good as new.

All reconstructive knee surgery falls into three categories: arthroscopy, open repairs, and replacements.

Arthroscopic surgery is not new, at least not in the Orient. Japanese surgeons have been experimenting with arthroscopy since 1918, even though they did not have video cameras, fiber-optic cables, or modern motorized tools. They worked with hand-held tools and primitive arthroscopes with lightbulbs attached at the end. Occasionally, these lightbulbs would break off inside the knee. The surgeon would then have to open the joint to get the lightbulb out—not a big plus! Because the instruments were primitive, the surgery could take hours—much longer than traditional open surgery. So arthroscopic surgery didn't catch on in the West until the early 1970s, and even then the surgery was mostly for diagnosis. But with the development of fiber-optic cables, motorized tools, and small video cameras that can be sterilized, much knee surgery can now easily be done arthroscopically. This has had a profound impact on the practice of knee surgery today. Up until the late seventies, if you needed surgery, you were admitted the night before the operation. Even for the smallest procedure, you would have a six-inch incision and would be sent home in a week or so. Then you would spend the next six weeks recovering from the trauma of the surgery.

Today almost 70 percent of knee surgery is done on an outpatient basis. You arrive in the morning, leave in the afternoon, and are never really admitted to the hospital. Because the incisions are about a $\frac{1}{4}$ inch long—just wide enough to admit an instrument the size of a knitting needle—the time it takes to recover is shortened. Usually you don't need crutches for more than a few days. Nevertheless, arthroscopic surgery has its limitations. Just like when a nail hole is plugged in a tire whose tread is badly worn, there are times when arthroscopy won't make much difference. The patients who do best following arthroscopic surgery have just one thing wrong with their knee: a bone chip or a torn piece of cartilage. The surgeon is treating the cause of the problem, not just a symptom. Once the bone chip or the torn flap of the meniscus is removed, the knee is as good as new.

By contrast, patients who have arthroscopic surgery for a painfully arthritic knee don't do as well. There may be a loose body or a torn piece of cartilage, but that is just part of a worn-out knee. Here the loose body is the effect of degenerative arthritis. By removing it, you are treating the effect, not the cause.

What *can* be accomplished with arthroscopic surgery? Originally the arthroscope was used for the diagnosis of internal derangements of the knee, torn cartilage, loose bodies, and the like. With the aid of the arthroscope, the surgeon can see the entire inside of the knee joint. First, the knee is filled with a fluid solution under pressure (the way you blow up a balloon), and then the inside of the distended joint is illuminated with a powerful light source directed into the joint by a fiber-optic cable.

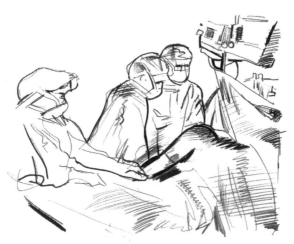

Arthroscopic procedure in the OR.

This enables the surgeon to see the synovial lining of the joint, evaluate inflammation, and, if necessary, biopsy the synovial membrane. Sometimes the biopsy is very helpful to the doctor in deciding whether it is a chronic inflammation or a chronic infection. The arthroscope is also used to probe the underside of the patella for the tell-tale pitting and softening of chondromalacia. The ends of the femur and tibia can be seen and probed for early signs of arthritis. If arthritis is discovered, its extent can be graded. With the arthroscope, the surgeon can see the entire meniscus on both sides of the joint and probe its substance for holes, rents, and tears. Both the anterior and posterior cruciate can be seen and, more important, tested for structural integrity. A cruciate ligament can be stretched to the point that it is no longer doing its job and yet still be there, like the worn-out waistband on an old pair of swimming trunks. Although the MRI has superseded arthroscopy for diagnostic purposes because it is noninvasive, arthroscopy is still the gold standard. The advance that arthroscopy has made possible has been in treating meniscal and ligament injuries. Now we no longer need to make a huge incision to treat these injuries and the rehabilitation is much shorter. Small flap tears can be trimmed and larger tears can be sutured with instruments no larger than knitting needles.

When does a physician decide to trim a meniscus rather than try to repair it? It comes down to whether there is enough blood supply in the area of the tear to allow the repair to heal. The surgeon can actually see the blood vessels on the surface of the meniscus and if the tear is in this vascularized zone, the repair will heal. Otherwise, the technique is to snip off the torn portion of the meniscus and leave the remaining normal piece in place.

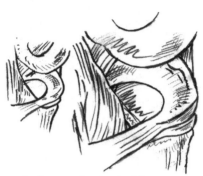

Arthroscopic meniscal repair.

Thirty years ago we used to remove every last piece of a torn meniscus, even the normal part. This was before the importance of the weight-bearing function of the meniscus was truly appreciated. As a result of the complete removal of the meniscus, most of these patients went on to develop arthritis.

The long-term results of selective, partial meniscectomies are much better. However, whenever possible, it is still best in the long run to repair a meniscus. Meniscal replacements and transplants are for the moment experimental and nothing is known about the long-term results. A meniscal replacement is made of synthetic material, whereas a meniscal transplant comes from an organ donor.

In the fifties and sixties, various suturing techniques were used to repair torn cruciate ligaments. Unfortunately, none of them worked. Since the seventies, torn cruciate ligaments have been reconstructed with tendons transferred from other parts of the patient's leg. (Tendon grafts can also be taken from organ donors at the same time that the heart, lungs, liver, and kidneys are harvested.) Originally the reconstruction was open-knee surgery, but now the tendon can be routed through tunnels in the knee and secured with screws to the tibia and femur with the aid of the arthroscope.

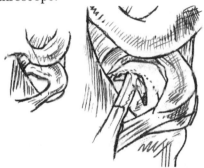

Arthroscopic partial menisectomy.

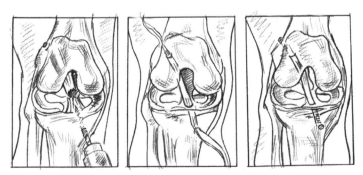

Arthroscopically assisted cruciate ligament.

The arthroscopic part of the procedure can be done through small incisions. A surgeon using the patient's own hamstring or patella tendon has to make an incision over the tendon in order to harvest it. This will leave a scar, but it is still much smaller than the old open reconstructions. When the doctor uses a cadaver graft, no such incision is needed and the whole operation can be done arthroscopically. The preferred method today is to use part of the patient's own patella tendon because of its reliability and safety.

The most commonly performed arthroscopic procedures are for removing bone chips, repairing torn menisci, and reconstructing torn ligaments. Patients who receive arthroscopic surgery for any of these problems have a 90 percent chance of a successful recovery.

Other things can be done with the arthroscope, but the success rate is not nearly as high. A tight patella can be released to relieve anterior knee pain, for instance. Or an arthritic knee can be debrided to remove spurs, which is like using a wire brush to get rid of rust on a hinge (you get rid of the loose rust but you still have a rusty hinge). About 60 to 70 percent of the patients who undergo this type of surgery are relieved of pain. Near the end of his carcer, Bobby Hull, the great 1960s hockey player, had several arthroscopic procedures to remove loose bodies from his knees so that he could establish the National Hockey League scoring record. Which he did. Until Wayne Gretzky smashed it in the 1980s.

❖ ❖ ❖

An old-fashioned but still useful open-knee surgical procedure is an osteotomy to straighten a malaligned and painful knee. Osteotomy means to cut a bone. Bowlegs are straightened by breaking the tibia below the knee and knock-knees are corrected by breaking the femur above the knee. The point of the surgery is to get the joint line parallel to the floor and redistribute the load evenly across the knee joint.

Nonetheless, not everyone with a bowleg has pain, and bowlegs and knock-knees that don't hurt should be left alone. Straightening a knee to prevent future trouble is visionary surgery that is just asking for trouble.

I did perform osteotomies on both knees of one patient, over the course of two operations. After the second, her husband jokingly observed that before her surgeries her legs were like an **O** and now they were like an **H**. I suppose that was a compliment. At any rate, her pain was gone and that was the point.

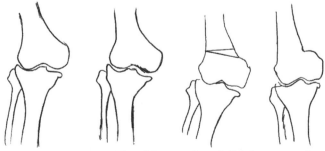

Mechanical principle of femoral and tibial osteotomies.

Unfortunately, an osteotomy has to be done through an incision and the patient has to wear a brace until the bones have healed. These operations are mainly done for pain relief and are usually effective for ten to fifteen years. Because the patient has already suffered joint damage, however, the results deteriorate with time. It is very much like realigning a tire that has already started to go bald—you will still get more mileage out of the tire if you realign it than if you don't. Osteotomies are most effective in young or middle-aged adults.

Knee replacements are most effective for patients who are over sixty and in pain. Years after he had retired from baseball, Mickey Mantle came to see me about his knees. His internist had sent him to see if he needed to have his knees replaced. Mantle told me that his knees were sore but he could play as much golf as he wanted and he didn't think he was in enough pain to warrant an operation. Furthermore, he said, Whitey Ford had had his knee replaced and couldn't do much more than he could before his surgery. In my view, Mantle was absolutely right. A knee replacement is to relieve pain, not to be able to play more golf.

The designs for knee replacements available today last about fifteen to twenty years before they wear out, which makes them appropriate for older patients. Since the average American lives to seventy-five, the knee is unlikely to wear out during the patient's lifetime.

Although we speak of replacing a knee, we are not

really replacing it. The end stage of both degenerative and rheumatoid arthritis is the destruction of the cartilage surface of the joint. What happens in replacement surgery is that the damaged and destroyed cartilage and adjacent bone is replaced with metal and plastic. The original knee-replacement devices were all metal, but these metal-on-metal models wore down much too quickly, usually within five years. Metal-on-plastic devices last much longer.

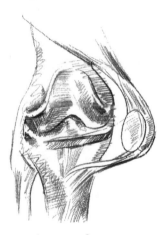

A knee replacement.

All the surfaces in the knee are replaced. The end of the femur is replaced with metal and the ends of the patella and tibia with plastic. Usually the metal is a chrome-cobalt steel. Steel has been used in the body to fix fractures since the thirties. The body does not react negatively to steel in the way it does to most other foreign bodies, such as wooden splinters or kidney transplants.

Once I treated a woman who had accidentally sat on a sewing needle that was left in the cushion of a club chair. The needle broke off just under the skin and over the next few weeks began to work its way toward the center of her knee joint. I had to remove the needle before it began to cause real damage to the nerves and blood vessels in its path. After the surgery, the woman told me that her husband had been a sheet-metal worker and that it was well known in his trade that wooden splinters worked themselves out but metal splinters worked their way in— meaning that the body rejects wooden splinters and not metal ones.

Knee-replacement devices can be cemented to the ends of the bone or the surfaces of the device can be treated so that the patient's bone will grow onto the surface of the device, locking it into the bone. Most knee replacements today use the former method, and all the long-term studies have been based on cemented devices. With cemented knee replacements, the failure from wear and loosening is about 7 to 10 percent over twenty years. The long-term results with uncemented designs is not known.

What can you expect from a knee replacement? As I mentioned, the most important reason to have a knee replacement is pain. About 90 percent of patients are relieved of their pain. But *not* right away, for this is major surgery! Everyone has pain for the first six weeks because of the incision. The next six weeks you are stretching out contracted scar tissue to get the range of motion back. During the surgery, the muscles take quite a beating, and during the next three months most patients experience thigh pain and fatigue after a long walk. By six months, most patients have little or no pain; they can now go up and down stairs, get in and out of a car, and walk as far as they want. Most patients can return to play golf and doubles tennis, but to expect to return to heavy-impact sports or contact sports is unrealistic. Nevertheless, because they had the operation for pain relief, most are quite satisfied with the outcome.

8

PREVENTION AND MAINTENANCE

What can you do to prevent injury? Well, it depends on what you want to do. It is like the old vaudeville joke about the man who turns up at his doctor's office, dangling his arm from his bent elbow, and saying, "It hurts when I do this." The doctor replies, "Well, then, *don't* do that." If you are like the father who hurt his knees carting his daughter's stuff down the dorm stairs, you might want to encourage your fit, aerobicized daughter to pitch in and help.

But if you are intent on engaging in your favorite seasonal sport, you can avoid injury without resorting to a stand-in or surrogate. In the off-season most people engaged in seasonal sports tend to get out of shape. For the average person a few weeks of preseason stretching and strengthening exercises will do the trick. The exercises should be both general and specific for the sport you intend to play.

General exercises are aerobic exercises. To get the best performance out of your muscles, your heart must provide oxygen and remove the metabolic waste products in an efficient and economical manner. Your heart must do this while it is being pushed to work harder and at a much faster rate than normal. The most efficient aerobic exercise is jogging, which in large part accounts for its popularity. Rowing, swimming, cycling, step exercises, and skipping rope are all equally good substitutes. In order for these activities to be of any aerobic value, you have to get your heart rate up to about 70 percent of its maximum rate. This target heart rate is about 150 beats per minute for the average adult (actually 220 minus your age—for instance, 220 minus 35). Twenty to thirty minutes of such activity for three times a week is sufficient for most sports. In the beginning of such a program you must exercise within your own tolerance limit. At the same time you have to overload your muscles if you expect to gain strength and endurance. At first you should go at a slow speed but for longer periods of time. You can jog for five minutes, walk for five minutes, and repeat; then, gradually increase the amount of time you run until you are running the entire twenty minutes. As you gain in strength, you can increase the speed and even reduce the amount of time of your workouts, or their frequency.

Warm-ups are important. The connective tissue of your muscles and ligaments is like taffy. It becomes more elastic as it warms up. This lets the joints loosen up and become more mobile. A loose joint is less likely to be injured than a stiff one. A warm muscle is more extensible than a cold one and can develop an explosive power that is very much like the elastic band on a slingshot. Remember that after a workout, a cool-down period is just as important. During vigorous exercise, your circulating blood is diverted to your muscles; the cool-down period is needed for your circulatory system to readjust this diversion in a more controlled fashion.

Specific exercises are designed to strengthen the muscles required for a particular sport. Here the strengthening program has to be combined with the skills required for the sport. Weight lifting is not enough to hit a baseball or a backhand in tennis. Strengthening must be combined with the practice of the movements necessary to develop the explosive power demanded by the sport. This explosive power is the ability to generate the maximum force at just the right time.

For all the competitive spirit they engender, racket sports are not that demanding aerobically. You spend a lot of time waiting for the other side to put the ball in play. Short bursts of energy are what is required. In preparation for the coming season, your time will be better spent on flexibility exercises and agility drills. A few times jogging around the court will suffice for the aerobic preparation. Short five-yard stop-and-start drills, lateral running, and back-up drills are more in order. Stretching the hamstrings, quadriceps, and calf muscles is very important.

The very common tennis injury "tennis leg" is a partial tear of the gastrocnemius muscle. It is caused by the sudden change in direction when a player is backing up, decides he has gone too far, and tries to go forward while he is still backpedaling. Fortunately, this injury will heal with time. A torn Achilles tendon is caused the same way, but it requires surgery to attach the completely separated ends of the tendon. The chance of these injuries happening can be reduced by pregame stretching exercises that make the muscles and tendons more elastic and less likely to rupture. Back-up drills help too. The real cause of a tennis elbow is getting to the ball too late and hitting a backhand behind you with your elbow and wrist bent, which tears the wrist extensor muscle. All the cortisone injections in the world won't help this. A combination of strengthening the wrist muscles and backhand drills is the answer.

Skiing is another seasonal sport that causes a lot of serious injuries. This sport relies on speed in conjunction with the long lever arm of the ski or ski pole. Again, it does not require aerobic preparation. To ski safely you need strength and endurance in your leg muscles—and the requisite skill. The main cause of skiing injuries is muscle fatigue as a result of poor conditioning and lack of that skill. (In fact, skiers are much more likely to be injured the first year they ski than later on.) In addition to tricky snow conditions, bad visibility, and poor conditioning, ill-fitting rental equipment is a big factor.

Falls and collisions account for most skiing injuries. Here common sense, supple ligaments, and strong muscles are your best defense against the two most common injuries in the leg: torn ligaments in the knee and fractured tibias. In preparation for skiing, strength training is essential. The most important element of a strength program is to overload the muscles with progressive resistance provided by free weights, weight machines, or the body's own weight in a regimen of push-ups, pull-ups, and toe raises. With each successive workout, try to increase the resistance or add another repetition. Ten repetitions is probably the right number. If you can't lift the weight at least eight times, the weight is too heavy. If you can lift it a dozen times, it is too light. This should be the guide for progressive resistance.

Intensity is important too. You should push yourself to the point of momentary exhaustion but not at the expense of the proper form. No fast or jerky movement. This is just asking for an injury. Greater gains in strength are made during the muscle-lengthening phase, so if it takes you two seconds to raise a weight, you should spend four seconds lowering it for the maximum benefit. Ten repetitions should take one minute. The best training routine is to allow a day's rest between workouts. With each workout, start with the largest muscles first—the quadriceps in the leg—in order to reach the necessary intensity. This same routine is just as important for such contact sports as football, soccer, rugby, and ultimate Frisbee.

If you are the recreational jogger who has been running two to three miles a day three times a week, mainly for health reasons, and you are bitten by marathon fever, long-distance training has its own special routines mainly focusing on endurance and heat training. Everyone has an intuitive sense of how to run, which is another reason that jogging is so popular: you don't need any special skill. Actually the elite marathon runners have learned to "shuffle" so that their center of gravity barely rises at all as they run. This saves an enormous amount of energy over these long races and gives them a tremendous advantage.

Specific stretching and strengthening exercises have been covered in chapter 3. If you intend to use weight machines, be sure to get instruction in their use from the trainer at your gym. With jogging, you are on your own. A few years ago in Rhode Island, cardiologists were studying a group of patients who had been put on a jogging program after suffering a heart attack. They wanted to see if there was an increased risk of a second heart attack with such a running program. A group of normal runners were included for comparison. No one died of a heart attack as a result, but several people in both groups were killed by cars. Running at dawn or dusk in dark clothing was the common denominator in these fatalities.

The advantage of a preseason conditioning program is that by increasing the strength of your muscles, ligaments, tendons, and bones, you will increase your flexibility, speed, and coordination and reduce the chance of injury. It is well worth the effort.

Finally, though, all the training and strengthening is just no substitute for common sense. Recently I saw a man in the office whose knees were killing him. He was trim and fit and went to a health club regularly, so he couldn't understand why his knees were acting up. As I was examining him, he mentioned that he lived in Westchester, worked in Manhattan, and had to be at work by 7:30 A.M. When I asked how he managed that, he told me with a straight face that for him it was a snap. He would get up at the last possible second and take the latest possible train to the city, so that he literally had to sprint to catch the train and then sprint from Grand Central Station to his workplace, some ten blocks away. No wonder his knees were killing him! He didn't need a better training program. He needed a new train schedule.

For most of us, knees are the things we scraped as kids, knobby excrescences that aren't particularly attractive. Unless they bother us, we don't think about them much. All the same, they are essential to our well-being. Their importance is underscored by numerous references to the knee joint in everyday speech: knee high, knee deep, knee jerk, knee socks, knee pants, housemaid's knee—not to mention nuns' knees and bees' knees. Now that you know what can happen to your knees and how fragile they are, perhaps you will put into practice some of the simple suggestions I have made in this book.

There is an old saying that goes: "When a man has married a wife, he finds out whether her knees and elbows are only glued together." The human body is a remarkable machine. No man-made engine could take the punishment that our joints absorb and keep functioning for some seventy-odd years. If you give them a little care and attention, they should last as long as you do.

INDEX

Ace bandage, 45, 53, 54, 55, 65
Achilles tendon, 90–91
Aerobic exercises, 44, 88–89
Agonist/antagonist, 16, 37
Anti-inflammatory drugs, 65, 69, 70, 71–71, 74
Apophyses, 42
Arthritis, 12, 43, 45, 46, 65–75, 78, 79, 80
Arthroscopy, 12, 13, 49, 76–82
Atrophy, 43, 53, 56, 62

Ballistic exercises, 30–31
Bleeding, 40, 47, 53, 54, 60
Bones, 19–27, 41, 47
Bowlegs, 58, 67, 83
Braces/bracing, 51, 53–58, 74, 84

Cartilage, 11, 22, 27, 28, 53, 66, 68, 75, 85
Casts, 43, 53
Chondromalacia, 41–42, 45, 46, 79
Chronic patella tendonitis, 44–45
Cold, application of, 59–60
Collagen, 22–23, 29
Compression, 23, 27, 45, 54
Conditioning exercises, 28–39, 93
Contrast bath, 62
Cortisone, 61, 72–73, 91
Cruciate ligaments, 12, 26, 41, 49–51, 79, 80–82
Crutches, 74, 77
Cryotherapy, 59–60
Cybex, 38–39, 64

Deformities, 68, 74
Degenerative arthritis (osteoarthritis), 65–67, 74, 75, 78, 85
Diathermy, 60–62

Electrical stimulation, 62–63

Endurance, 31, 32–34, 37, 39, 53, 64, 89
Exercises, 53, 63–64, 74, 88–90; see also under specific kinds

Femur, 14, 15, 19, 20–22, 23, 24, 26, 27, 48, 51, 57–58, 79, 81, 83, 85
Fibrinogen, 40, 49, 50
Flexion contracture, 74
Fractures, 20, 47, 52, 56, 85

Gamma globulin, 69–70
Gastrocnemius, 30, 90
Gout, 72

Hamstring muscles, 16–18, 30, 90
Heat application, 59, 60–62, 74
Hyaline cartilage, 22
Hydrotherapy, 59, 62

Ice, 44, 45, 47, 54, 59–60, 65
Immobilization, 42–43, 52, 53–54, 56–57
Immune system, 68, 69–70, 71
Impact absorption, 18, 46
Impact loads/loading, 14, 22, 23, 35, 38, 45, 46, 64, 67
Inflammatory arthritis, 65, 67–71, 74
Injuries, 10–13, 40–52, 53, 65–66
Iontophoresis, 62
Isokinetic training, 38–39, 64
Isometric exercise, 31–34, 37, 39, 45
Isotonic exercise, 31, 34–35, 37, 63

Jogging, 39, 89, 90, 92–93
Joints, 68, 69, 84
Jumper's knee, 43, 44–45

Knee joint, 8, 12, 14–27, 46
Kneecap; see Patella (kneecap)
Knock-knees, 58, 67, 83

Ligament injuries, 29, 40, 49–51, 56, 79, 80–81
Ligaments, 12, 24–27, 28, 47, 53, 66, 91
Lymphocytes, 70–71

Maintenance, 13, 88–94
Malalignment, 66–67, 83
Massage, 59, 62
Medicines, 12–13, 69
Meniscal replacements and transplants, 12, 80, 82
Meniscus, 11, 21, 22, 23–24, 41, 47, 48–49, 66, 77, 79–80
Motion, restoring, 53, 59, 60, 63
Muscle contraction, 24, 29, 34, 38, 46–47
Muscle spasms, 53, 58, 59, 60
Muscle strains, tears, 28–29, 40
Muscles, 15–18, 27, 28, 31, 42, 46, 54–55, 58, 63, 91–92; see also Atrophy
Musculoskeletal system, 14

Nautilus system, 37–38, 39
Neoprene knee sleeve, 44, 46, 54–55

Osgood-Schlatter disease, 42–44
Osteotomy, 83–84

Pain, 12, 41–42, 45–46, 47–48, 53, 58, 59, 63, 64, 82
Pain medications, 47–48, 74
Pain relief, 65, 82, 84, 86–87
Patella (kneecap), 19–20, 41, 47, 55, 79, 82
Patella straps, 44
Patella tendons, 42–43, 44–45, 82
Phonophoresis, 61, 62
Physical therapists, 59
Prevention, 88 94
Progressive resistance exercises, 34–37, 38, 91–92
Proprioceptors, 18–19
Prostaglandins, 70, 72
Protective mobilization, 54
Proteoglycans, 22–23

Quadriceps muscle, 14, 16–17, 19,
26, 30, 43–44, 46–47, 90, 92
Quadriceps tendon, 43, 47

Recreational sports, 28–29, 39, 51
Replacements, 12, 13, 66, 76, 84–87
Resistive exercises, 31–39, 64
Rest, 44, 45, 54, 65, 74
Rheumatoid arthritis, 68–71, 72, 85
Rheumatoid factor, 69–70
Running, 10, 41, 44, 92–93

Skiing, 11, 21, 26, 28, 51, 91–92
Splints/splinting, 53–54, 56, 74
Sports, 12, 17–18, 25, 28–29, 40, 51, 88
Stair climbing, 11, 14, 15, 41, 45
Strength, 31, 32, 34, 37, 39, 53, 64, 89
Strength training, 91–92
Strengthening, 63–64
Strengthening exercises, 29, 31–39, 51, 88, 90, 93
Stretching, postexercise, 63
Stretching exercises, 29–31, 39, 88, 91, 93
Surgery, 9, 12, 13, 47, 51–52, 76–87, 91
Swelling, 27, 40–41, 47, 53, 54, 58, 59, 60, 62
Synovial lining, 24, 40, 79

Tendon grafts, 81, 82
Tendons, 24, 31, 42, 44–45, 46, 53
Tennis elbow, 91
"Tennis leg," 90
Tibia, 14, 15, 17, 19, 22, 23, 24, 26–27, 48, 51, 57–58, 79, 81, 83, 85
Twisting, 21, 23, 50

Variable resistance programs, 31, 37–38
Viscoelasticity, 29

Weight lifting, 34–35, 37, 38, 39, 63, 90, 91
White blood cells, 60, 70–71, 72